Kirk's
Poetry

Kirk's Poetry

Kirk Philipsen

ARPress
ILLUMINATING IDEAS.
EMPOWERING VOICES

ARPress
45 Dan Road Suite 5
Canton MA 02021
Hotline: 1(888) 821-0229
Fax: 1(508) 545-7580

Ordering Information:
Quantity sales. Special discounts are available on quantity purchases by corporations, associations, and others. For details, contact the publisher at the address above.

Printed in the United States of America.

ISBN-13:	Softcover	979-8-89356-404-4
	eBook	979-8-89356-403-7

Library of Congress Control Number: 2024902528

Table of Contents

CHAPTER ONE..1

    Christian Poems

CHAPTER TWO... 13

    Christian Poems that are now on my new CD, "Kirk In Spirit"

CHAPTER THREE 20

    Poems about children

CHAPTER FOUR 26

    Poems of Love, or a dream Love

CHAPTER FIVE... 30

    Fun Poems on how Country songs are made

CHAPTER SIX... 39

    About my son Christopher and the dedication of this book to him About the Author

TO EVERYTHING THERE IS A SEASON
(Ecclesiastes 3, 1-8)

A time for every purpose under heaven;
A time to be born, a time to die;
A time to plant, and a time to pluck what has been planted;
A time to kill, and a time to heal;
A time to break down, and a time to build up;
A time to weep, and a time to laugh;
A time to mourn, and a time to dance;
A time to cast away stones, and a time to gather stones;
A time to embrace, and a time to refrain from embracing;
A time to gain, and a time to lose;
A time to keep, and a time to throw away;
A time to tear, and a time to sew;
A time to keep silence, and a time to speak;
A time to love, and a time to hate;
A time of war, and a time of peace.

We all have to go through our seasons, but let's not let them be our stumbling block. The Lord will guide us through the seasons, if we give them to Him, and have faith that He will be there to help us to conquer our battles, and win the war for us.

CHAPTER ONE

These are some poems that the Lord gave me in 1982

A BAD DAY

If anything could go wrong, it went wrong today,
The pain grew stronger, and more troubles came.
As though in the desert, I feel stranded and alone,
It seems God has left me, in this battle on my own.
My armor is stripped, my sword not drawn,
All possible protection, it seems now gone.
Down to the lowest, I've truly tried my best,
But all roads I see, lead to certain death.
As my heart begins to melt, and death enters my bones,
A small light of hope, from the Lord is shown.
And with that hope, knowing the Lord is near,
My senses become clearer, for a message to hear.
Life comes back, into my bones again,
I realize now, hey this isn't the end.
With that little bit of hope, I've come alive,
Trusting the Lord, I was willing to die.

A FAMILY IN CHRIST

I praise You Father, for my family in Christ,
For all the love they give, without thinking twice.
The prayers they speak, all the support they bring,
Their spiritual gifts, that teach everything.
The wisdom the knowledge, that You've given us,
In each other with love, we can trust.
I praise You Father, for making me a part,
Of one of Your family, from the very start.
Please bless my brothers and sisters in Christ,
And for Your redemption, that can't be bought at any price.

I PRAISE YOU FOR BEING TRUE

Dear Lord Jesus, You know how I feel,
The love in my heart, for You is real.
Thank You for Your comfort, and giving my soul peace,
And upon me Jesus, Your Spirit You release.
And I praise You Lord, for all that You do,
I praise You Lord, for being true.

HUMBLE

As you turn your head, soften your heart,
Praise the Lord, and satan shall depart.
Speak of the love, that God sends us,
Spread it abundantly, and in the Lord do trust.
Always keep peace, on your mind and heart,
From your mind and soul, God's Word shouldn't part.
If you show others, the love given to you,
The example you set, as a Christian is true.

WE KNOW HE'S THERE

Even though there's clouds, and the sun does hide,
And the moon and stars, are on the other side,
You can't see them, but they still exist,
On the other side, of the cloudy mist.
And deep in the forest, a tree does fall,
And there's no one around, to hear it at all.
But it still makes a noise, as it crashes to the ground,
Even if there is nothing, to hear the sound.
Man was created, a long time ago,
We didn't see it, but we know it's so.
The earth was made, out of the vastness of space,
We didn't see it, but we are on the place.
Everything God created, everything in the air,
We didn't see Him, but we know He is there.

HEAVENLY FATHER

Oh heavenly Father, I praise You so,
For Your son Jesus, that we know.
The eternal light, in our hearts does shine,
That small path to heaven, we surely did find
Because of Your grace, and Your everlasting love,
You've given us hope, from Your spirit above.
Hold me Father, and bless Your loving Son,
And I pray Your gracious spirit, will enter each and everyone.
And to Jesus Christ, in whom I'll stray never,
Always be the glory, forever and ever.

BLESSED BE THE CHILDREN

I praise You Father, for Your blessed children,
That are so pure and full of love.
They are so clean and have no evil.
Like the whiteness of Your dove,
Weak and frail and soft and warm, Is the blessed child.
With pure of minds, and pure of hearts,
And nothing that is defiled.
You show Your love through a child,
And it fills our hearts with joy,
To be blessed by You, in this world,
With a baby girl, or a boy.
Oh how I wish we could be,
As if we all were babes,
So pure of heart, and clear of minds,
Like we first were made.
I love You Father, with all my heart,
And I praise You for the child,
And pray to You for the babes,
And let them not be defiled.

NOW HE'S FIRST

And there was the Lord, in the backyard of my heart,
In the back of my mind, at the end of the chart.
A one on the scale, where the highest is ten,
And everyone but Him, was my closest friend.
Then coming from the depths, of my empty soul,
Was a cry of love, and the truth was told.
He came through me, like a gushing well,
A feeling of peace, was starting to swell.
Then I blew up, and my body was lame,
Like the still of the waters, and the morning after rain.
And I saw Jesus, as He carried me,
Like He had in the past, but I didn't see.

Now He is there, for eternal time,
First in my heart, and first on my mind.
I see Your eternal light, Your everlasting love,
As I hope for my eternity, to be with You above.

KEEP MY SOUL

Take away Lord Jesus, my boastful pride,
Release the evil, that's inside.
Take the sovereignty, and cast it away,
Let me live for You, every single day.
Don't turn Your eyes, away from me,
Please hear my cries, from way down deep.
Listen to my heart, for it sings for You,
Songs of praise, in everything I do.
Heal my heart, help me with this song,
Guide me to righteousness, please keep me from wrong.
Oh listen to me, Son of God,
Teach me Your ways Lord, with Your powerful rod.
Give me Your armor, and make me bold,
And I ask in Your name Jesus, that You keep my soul.

I CAN WALK

I cry every day, and I sit in shame,
Hating myself, because I am lame.
I wait by a pond, for an angel the Lord to send,
So maybe I can crawl there, and be the first to get in.
But others get there, before I can get near,
I may never be healed, that's my greatest fear.
But who is this man, who I can hear talk?
Saying "sin no more, take up your pallet, and walk".
I felt such warmth, as this man talked,
I immediately got up, and I walked.
I shouted for joy, all through the land,
Oh wait, I failed to get the name of that man.

WE PRAISE YOU FATHER

Oh Father Lord of hosts, how majestic You are.
We want to glorify You Lord, with all of our hearts.
With a voice like thunder, and only You we fear,
You took away our blindness, and let us hear,
About Your kindness, and Your righteousness,
And all Your armor, You provide for us.
Oh praise You Father, our precious loving Lord,
Oh praise You Father, we can't ask for more.
Like footprints in the sand, You carry us through our mourn,
When our troubles oppress us, You calm the storm.
You made us the seasoning, the salt of the world,
The lighthouse by the sea, when the waters are hurled.
But You are the only, true living Light,
That pierces the darkness, in the darkest of night.
Oh praise You dear Father, may all the glory be to You,
Oh praise You dear Father, for being so true.
Oh praise You Father, for Your loving ways,
We will praise You Father, with our hearts ablaze.
Through eternity our Lord, we want You to know,
That is how long Lord, we will praise You so.

HIS LOVE

Just as the stars, shine bright above,
Just as bright for us, is our Lords love.
The kindness He gives, He gives abundantly,
The compassion in His heart, is for you and me.
The glory of God, is upon the whole earth,
And it's been there always, before any birth.
He is a gracious Lord, and He loves us so,
With the mercy He shows us, that's how we know.
Thank You Jesus, for all that You give,
And the eternal life, that Your children will live.

TO YOU LORD

This is from me Jesus, sincerely to You,
I want to thank You, for all that You do.
Here's from my heart Lord, that's open and bare,
So You can see all the love for You, that is there.
The tears in my heart, You've seen them I know,
Enough love to You, I can't seem to show.
I want to hold You, and cry at Your feet,
Begging that my adversary, soon You'll defeat.
Hold me dear Jesus, let me cry all night,
So when I've finished, I'll see Your path of light.
So forever I can please You, and never again sin,
And serve You and love You, forever, amen.

KEEP ME

Father please keep in my heart, all the love I have for You
Let nothing but praise come from my lips, and from my heart it's true.
Keep me busy serving You, every day and night,
Forgive me of all my sins, and keep me on the path that's right.
Everything that I do Lord, let it be glory to You,
Lift me up and send me Your spirit, so I serve You in all that I do.
I love You so for choosing me, and opening up my eyes,
And through the glorious spirit of Your word,I'm in Your precious light.
Give me strength oh Father of love, to see Your righteous path,
To resist the evil in the world, that sets ablaze Your wrath.
Keep me humble oh my Lord, and I pray upon my knees,
That Your love pours in my heart, that I so badly need.
I love You so my precious Lord, and from the bottom of my heart,
I pray You hold me in Your arms, and from You I'll never part.

THANK YOU FATHER

We thank You Father, for the blessings You give,
And how You show us, that Your Son does live.
Your power overall, below and above,
Your spirit of truth, Your abundant love,
Praise His name, oh praise the Lord.
You brought the light, and You guide the sword.
Praise the Lord, oh praise His holy name,
You show us so much love, and we want to do the same.
The blind now see, and the lame do walk,
The ones who were speechless, now joyfully talk.
Because of the name, of Jesus Christ,
All those people healed, have come to Your light.
Praise the Lord, oh praise His holy name,
You show us so much love, and we want to do the same.

HE'S THE LIGHT OF LIGHT

As the sun in the morning, slowly shows it's glory,
It brightens the day, and reveals God's story.
The power of the water, as it builds a wave,
Just one word from God, makes the water stay.
Glory to our savior, who controls the light,
He's the only way, to escape the night.
He is the creator, He even made the sun,
With all of it's glory, and even it's light is second to one.
The light of Jesus, is the light of all light,
And He is your light, in the darkest of night.

REJOICE

Let's lift our hands, to our Lord Jesus,
To show what He's done, really does please us.
Let's bow our hearts, and give Him praise,
For His Holy Spirit, in us that prays.
Shout with joy, rejoice my friend,
For Jesus released us, from our bondage of sin.
He's shown compassion, and mercy and grace,
Upon all His children, who give Him praise.
Clap your hands, and shout for joy,
Cleanse your hearts, as of a baby boy.
Give Jesus your heart, let Him cast out your sins,
Pray to the Lord Jesus, to please come in.
Let Jesus guide you, both day and night,
And your loving God, will give you eternal life.

I WANT TO PLEASE YOU

Please help me Lord, I cry out to You,
I want so badly, to do what pleases You.
Take my sovereignty, and my sins away,
Give me Your freedom, this very day.
For in my heart, You know I love You,
I want to do Your will, in all that I do.
I exalt You Lord, and praise Your name,
And all my iniquities, are all my blame.
Oh help me Father, I cry out to You,
I want so badly, to do what pleases You.

NIGHT

As the day turns into night, and our spirit becomes the prey,
We put on our armor of God, and rebuke temptations away.
The evil thoughts the seductive eyes, the whispering in the streets,
The luring looks the skimpy clothes, the smell of perfume reeks.
Stay at home and lock your doors if you don't have your armor on right,
For you have to have the strongest of faith, to even start to pierce the night.

PAIN

Hold my heart, oh Father of love,
Send me Your spirit, from the heavens above.
Give me strength Lord, to withstand this pain,
As my whole-body aches, with feelings of shame.
My spirit is drifting, which fills my soul with fear,
That my pleading cries, You will not hear.
Deliver me oh Lord, from this awful pain,
Before I go completely, into eternal shame.
Grab up my enemies, oh God of wrath,
Deliver me oh Lord, unto Your righteous path.vww
Fill me with light, and make me bold,
Death takes my body, but Jesus takes my soul.

HERE ARE SOME LIGHTNING BOLT THROWING POEMS THAT I HAD FUN WITH

THE WRATH OF GOD

You can hide anywhere you want, and flee both night and day,
You can cover up your feelings, and think your evil ways,
But even a serpent can't find a hole, deep enough to hide,
The fear of God that he has, bound up inside.
There's not a demon or a man, with his sinful ways,
That can crawl far enough, from God's judgment day,
To be bound in chains, and cast away,
And receiving awful grief,
Where there will be weeping, and gnashing of teeth.
In the darkest dark, and the deepest deep,
You never will die, You'll have eternal grief,
So if you don't change your ways, don't think that it's odd,
The torcher you'll go through, come the wrath of God!

FIRE PIT

How dare you say that you're a godly man,
When you curse the power, of God's right hand.
You look with lust, at your neighbors wife,
And turn and tell me you have eternal life?
You say you're saved, and a righteous man,
Then you steal from your brother, anything you can.
You get in fights, and drink of wine,
Let me tell you brother, you are blind.
Repent you sinners, and give up your life,
Turn to Jesus, for your eternal light.
Ask our Lord to forgive you of your sins,
Or in the great pit of fire, eternally you'll spend.

ARE YOU SAVED

Oh how wicked you are, the Lord helps you and shows you grace,
You speak of righteousness, and then curse Him to His face.
Drunkenness and slandery, and lust within your heart,
Then you enter Gods house, and boast how good you are.
Oh you hypocrites, how surprised you'll be,
When you're to enter heaven, and the Lord rebukes thee.
Get on your knees, and beg and cry,
Ask for forgiveness, pluck out your eyes.
For don't you know, when this world shall end,
That you won't enter heaven, unless you're born again?
And your fleshly body, so full of sin,
Has to die, and with baptism be cleansed.
The Holy Spirit, must enter your heart,
And with Gods grace, eternal life will start.

PRAYER

As the day begins, and you look to the heavens,
Pray to your loving God, from the begging until the day ends.
You can't pray, only once a week,
And have God's blessings, or hear Him speak.
He wants your heart, and all of your love,
He wants your thoughts all ways, to be on the heavens above.
Don't be so selfish, and seek all your wants,
Don't think of desires, rebuke them at once.
If you all ways keep, your mind on the Lord,
And fear your God, and His flashing sword.
What's more important, you or Him?
If you think it's yourself, you're living in sin.

CHAPTER TWO

Here are some poems the Lord gave me in 1982 that have been written as songs, which are now my new Christian praise CD "KIRK IN SPIRIT"

It has been over 20 years, I have always done these songs on an acoustic guitar with some harmonies on the vocals. But now the Lord has given me the lead, rhythm, and bass parts on the guitars, also the harmonies on the vocals. And there is a lot more extras that make the songs a lot better. These songs can be heard on the links I provided in this book.

BESIDE YOU

When your heart has melted, and your bones do weep,
You have this feeling of emptiness, way down deep.
Your body cries out, and pleads for a cure,
What is it your seeking, your not sure,
Troubles in your path, everywhere you go,
You're life is falling apart, you know it's so.
Now stop for a moment, and open up your eyes,
Look there beside you, as Jesus cries,
He's always been there, to help you along,
But you never did see Him, through all your wrong.
Now His tears, are tears of glee,
Because finally, His compassion you did see,
Open up your heart, let Jesus in,
And your sorrows soon will end.
Now stop for a moment, and open up your eyes,

Look there beside you as Jesus cries,
He's always been there, to help you along,
But you never did see Him, through all your wrong.

HIS GENTLE TOUCH

Just as the dew, falls gently on the land
So is the touch, of our Lord's hand
He shows His love to us everyday
The way only He can, in such a special way.
As the butterfly, is His gentle kiss
The feeling of His peace, in the morning mist
The quiet gentle setting, of the sun
A babbling creek, from the snow does run
The first cry, from a new baby boy
Fills so many hearts, with Gods loving joy
The Lord is loving, and He shows us everyday
Just look around you, and marvel in His ways.

LORD OF MY LIFE

Jesus is the Lord, of my life
In my darkest hour, He's my light
He's my every breath that I take
He's my every move, that I make
He's my strength, when I need to run
He's my love, when I need to love someone

I KNOW I'M SAVE

I know that Jesus is Lord, and that God raised Him from the dead
It's not by works that I'm saved, It's by His love and His grace
I know I'm saved because I called upon his name

And through God's word, I'm saved
I call upon the name of the Lord
I call upon the name of the Lord
I know I'm saved because I called upon His name
And through God's word, I'm saved
The price has already been paid, through the blood of the lamb
His gift to us is eternal life, and all we gotta do is call on His name
I know I'm saved because I called upon His name
And through God's word, I'm saved
I call upon the name of the Lord
I call upon the name of the Lord
I know I'm saved because I called upon His name
And through God's word, I'm saved.

LIFE OF THE LIGHT

My dear sweet Jesus, I love You so
And with Your blessings, I grow and grow
I'm like a vapor that's blown away
You pick me up in Your arms to stay
We are Your children, and we love You so
You've written the word, so we will know
You died on the cross for our sins
Now it is time that we're born again
My dear sweet Jesus, I want you to know
From the bottom of my heart, I praise You so
You are the glory, the great Shepard of the sheep
When I see what You've done for me I want to weep
You are the glorious life of the light
You took my darkness, and made it so bright
Now please forgive me of all my sins
With the blood that You shed, I'm born again.

UNTO YOU (I GIVE)

You opened my eyes, to see Your precious face
And brought forth Your spirit, to see Your loving grace
I give to You, my deepest love
My heart to hold, in Your heart above
Unto You I give all my praise, unto You I glorify
Unto You I lift up my heart, and it's You I praise
You heal the sick, and give us life
The blind now see, Your morning light
The deaf now hear, the rain that falls
Everything that's created You've created it all
Unto You I give all my praise, unto to You I glorify
Unto You I lift up my heart, and it's You I praise.

WHEN YOUR HEART HAS JESUS

As the spirit ascends from heaven, and livens up your soul
To open up your heart, so we can achieve Gods goals
To feed the hungry spirit, and quench the thirsty mind
And eternal life with Jesus, for every one to find
So if you feel a hunger, and your soul does thirst
All your troubles will leave you, if you except Jesus first
Yes He does love us so, and forgives us of our sins
And when your heart has Jesus, your new life begins.

WITH YOU

Take these sins of mine, wash them away
Cleanse this soul of mine, so I can stay
In the light You made for me
There I'll always want to be with You.
You made my life complete, I praise You so

You're all I'll ever need, I want You to know
That I want to serve You in every way
So that I can always stay, with You

THE WRATH OF GOD

You can hide anywhere you want, and flee both night and day
You can cover up your feelings, and think your evil ways
But even a serpent can't find a hole, deep enough to hide
The fear of God that he has, bound up inside
There's not a demon or a man, with his sinful ways
That can crawl far enough, from God's judgment day
To be bound in chains and cast away
And receiving awful grief
Where there will be weeping, and gnashing of teeth
In the darkest dark, and the deepest deep
You never will die, you'll have eternal grief
So if you don't change you ways, don't think that it's odd
The torcher you'll go through, come the wrath of God!

Here are some other poems that are now songs

THE MEADOW OF YOUR MIND

As I drift through the meadow of your mind, a peace I find within you
Brings your sunshine into my heart, with white clouds and skies of blue
I saw the love you had within, and it made me cry
Knowing how happy we could be, you and I
I saw you riding through the meadow, your hair flowing in the breeze
The sun caught your glow, and you looked like an angel to me
I always see you from far away, and so radiant you seem
Are you my real love, or are you just a dream
If you are just a dream, I hope I don't wake up
I need to show you how much I love you, and because of you I won't give up

You're the only one, that's brought sunshine in my life
So please be there, in my dreams tonight
You're the only one, that's brought sunshine in my life
So please be there, in my dreams tonight.

I GOTTA PERFECT PHOTOGRAPHIC MEMORY OF YOU

I gotta perfect photographic memory of you
I know exactly what you stand for, and everything that you do
You got that perfect little body, and the prettiest face too
And if you ever take me back hon, I picture what we're gonna do
I go down to the local pub, and yeah I have a drink or two
I see alotta pretty girls there, but none of them compare to you
You got that perfect little body, and the prettiest face too
I gotta perfect photographic memory of you
I hope you don't get the wrong picture, of the reason I left you
It had nothing to do with me babe, back there in 92
But when you left me for my best friend, I didn't know what to do
And now I've forgiven your past girl, I picture just me and you
I gotta perfect photographic memory of you
I know exactly what you stand for, and everything that you do
You got that perfect little body and the prettiest face too
I gotta perfect photographic memory of you
Well I keep thinking you'll come back
Well I guess I'm on the wrong track
Must be something that I lack
I guess it must be you
I gotta perfect photographic memory of you
I know exactly what you stand for, and everything you do
You got that perfect little body, and the prettiest face too
I gotta perfect photographic memory of you.

A CERTAIN THING FOR YOU

I like my morning coffee
Afternoon I like to sip my tea
But late at night I want
Someone like you for me
I know you don't know me very well
But at times I'm sure you can tell that,
You know I gotta certain thing for you
So why don't we just get acquainted
There's a picture that needs to be painted cause,
You know I gotta certain thing for you
There's not a lot for me to say
Except I want you everyday cause,
You know I gotta certain thing for you
All my love is what I'll pay
To be with you everyday cause,
You know I gotta certain thing for you
Yes, you know I gotta certain thing for you.

CHAPTER THREE

MOM DAD AND ME

We were so happy, mom, dad, and me,
Loving each other forever, endlessly.
We worked as a family, to have a happy home,
Mom, dad, and me together, hardly ever alone.
Oh how I loved it just mom, dad, and me,
Loving each other forever, endlessly.
Life was so wonderful, at five for me,
We loved each other, mom, dad, and me.
Till one day, my daddy left home,
Leaving my mommy, and me alone.
What did I do to make daddy leave?
Did I say something to daddy, that I didn't mean?
Is there something I can do, what would it take?
What can I say, to stop this heartache?
Oh how I loved it, just mom, dad, and me,
Loving each other forever, endlessly.
Now daddy's with someone, and mommy's with someone,
And I don't understand, why I don't have anyone.
Every night I get down on my knees,
And pray to God, for mom, dad, and me.
I ask you God, please bring daddy home,
So I won't feel, so all alone.
Make it like it was, when we were so happy,
Loving each other, mom, dad, and me.
Oh how I loved it, just mom, dad, and me,
Loving each other, endlessly,
Loving each other, endlessly.

GIRL OF THREE

We walked through the valley
The smell of flowers, and grass so sweet
Touching a piece of heaven
Floating on the freedom, that was beneath our feet
The warmth of our hearts, that made it such a beautiful day
The love that surrounded us, nobody could ever take that away
Green, green grass, and the trees reaching so tall
We could hear the silence of the gentle breeze
Across the meadow, that's all
I turned to see, her hair glistening in the sun
Flowing long
And bouncing as she run
Then I realized
I loved her, and she loved me
How precious it is
To have a little girl that's three.

SHOT

Every child leaves for school
Feeling that they are a fool
To even walk down the street
Not knowing who they'll see or meet
Children go to school for the fun
They know they have to learn
But at school, it's to play and run
They tell us, I don't want to go to school today
And we often wonder why
They tell us they are sick
Or their homework they can't find
Do we really know
The reason they don't want to go?
Why they act sick in the morning
Or why they move so slow?

Son, I said, what is the problem?
He said, dad, you really don't know
Yes I do son
So hurry get ready to go
No, listen to me dad
Let me tell you about yesterday
My friend brought a gun and said to me
Come on, let's go play
I told him no, like you've taught me
He said, don't worry it's not loaded
And this is between you and me
I stayed back as he walked ahead
And twirled the gun with clout
But when the gun went off, someone was down
He said, say nothing so no one will find out
I've found out that a lot of kids in school
Either carry guns, or a knife
I really don't want to go to school
Cause dad, I fear my life
Even on a bus they watch
What is their destiny
Can't they even learn today?
Instead of the fear, of what they might see.

YOUR CHILDREN

Having a child, is the most important thing you can do,
Receiving their heart, and life too.
So special, so loving, so innocent are they,
Hold them keep them, love them every single day,
You will never know what will happen,
While a busy life you live,
Take time out, for your precious little kids.
Because you may wake up some day,
And find that one of them is gone,
You will wonder the rest of your life,
What did I do wrong?

Knowing that maybe, you could have stopped,
The death of your child.
Once they are gone,
You well never again, see them smile.
Hold them love them, for they're only kids,
Hold them love them, for they're your children,
And not just kids.

SO YOUNG SO PURE

The memory of meeting you, so young so pure,
I had to talk to you softly, whispering in your ear.
You brought joy, to everyone around you,
Your smile, your spirit, everyone knew,
How much love, that you had inside.
And at two months old, you made me feel alive.
We laughed, we played, even did rhythm and blues.
And son I loved how, you played those old spoons.
You brought light, into everyone you met,
And if it ever were a movie, I think the stage was set.
You were the main actor, and you deserved it all,
And you still are today son, within us all.
Learning how to ride a bike, was fun for you and me,
Baseball, football, soccer, you did all of them with ease
The girls, the pizza, the music and school,
Doing your homework, following the rules.
You held your ground, and took your stand,
Against all that teased you, and made you small.
Through all your love, you taught them all.
All that met you, knew your love and your smile,
They knew you loved hugs, in their hearts, it's on file.
And we know He took you, and I know it was right.
Your with Him now, and you deserve it so well,
All the love you gave, we love you son, farewell.
We talk, we laugh, we think about you,
We miss you so much son, but we can't sing the blues.
We know where you're at son, and that's in a different place,

Because you're with the Lord now, that's something we can't replace.
He is the best thing that ever happened to us all,
He saw you standing, it was His beckoned call,
For you to be by His side,
Knowing someday, we would take the ride,
Not that it's something we know,
But trying so hard, to be by You, it shows.
So young, so pure, in hearts you'll stay,
We've tried so hard, God has His ways.
So young, so pure, so loving at heart,
So young, so pure, you have done your part.
You made us happy, you're so hard to forget,
So young, so pure, your death we regret.

MY LIFE, MY LOVE, NOW GONE

What a joy it was, with you in my life,
So young so pure, and a spirit so right.
Three pounds at birth, you fought and strived,
They didn't think you would make it, but you survived.
A will to live, what a little man you were,
Through the needles and the probing, your heart endured.
And then I met you, so small so strong,
You made it through that, what could ever go wrong?
As I helped raise you, it was quite a task,
Sick all the time, I didn't think I could last.
But your mother was there, to help us through,
The hard times we had, her, me, and you.
As you grew up, and started school,
The things you went through, were so very cruel.
But you always had a smile, on your face,
No matter what happened, you kept your place.
You fought, you struggled, through life from the start,
We never gave up, we knew you would go far.
Everyone loved you, and you gave them your heart,
Your smiles, your hugs, you set everyone apart.
You made friends every place you went,

And we as parents, knew you were heaven sent.
Then one day you told me, about the pains you had,
We went to the doctor, and they told me it was bad.
You said, don't worry dad, I'll be alright,
But would you please stay with me, for tonight?
And I told you son, I will always be here,
And you said thanks dad, I just want you near.
Oh dad what is it, why do I feel so weak?
I said, son don't worry God's on your side, He won't leave.
He's right there beside you, right or wrong,

You know I love you, and so does He.
Put your trust in Him, now let's sing Him a song.
My life, my love, now gone,
Yes he was my life, my love, and now he is gone.

REJOICE WITH ME

To all of you who have read
The poem about my son
We can't change the past
Or undo what's been done
We can only hope and pray
That the Lord will help us to understand
The way things have to happen
To fulfill His eternal life plan
So let's not sorrow
Please come and rejoice with me
For my son is alive
With our Lord Jesus, eternally.

CHAPTER FOUR

LIKE AN ANGEL

As bright as the sunshine,
Is your smile to me,
Like opening a present,
Children light up with glee.
Like the dew on the roses,
And the morning dawn,
So is a moment with you.
Like nothing is ever wrong,
The glow you have,
The way you light up a day,
For everyone that meets you,
And anyone that comes your way.
You come once in a lifetime,
You are one of a kind,
The gift you have with people,
Is so hard to find.
I feel sorry for people,
Who's heart you haven't touched,
But you touched mine,
That's why I love you so much.

MY HEART GOES OUT TO YOU (MY SON)

You were so young, and knew your life was so right,
An adult in your mind, and you fought a good fight.
Knowing your ways, knowing your mind,
I didn't want to stop you, because of the truth you'd find.

Growing up isn't easy, but son we try,
To make your life better, and I know you'll be fine.
You've been through a lot, and I know the pain,
But we're still here to teach you, through cloudy days and the rain.
We've been through so much, we've seen it all,
My heart goes out to you, I know you won't fall.
I'm here to catch you, you are the love of my life,
I'm here to catch you every day and night.
Don't forget I love you, and I always will,
You are like a rainbow, in every heart you fill.
With love and laughter, and your heart so true,
I want to tell you, my heart goes out to you.

FRIEND OR LOVER

We've always been friends,
We've been so close, you and I,
And I hope it stays that way,
Until the day that we die.
We help each other,
Through the good and the bad,
We even hold each other,
When the other is sad.
Through the sorrow and the hurt,
You have always been there.
And the loss and the sadness,
With me you always share.
I hold you I comfort you,
When you're really down,
And when you need a loving friend,
You know I'm always around.
You lost your love,
Just the other night,
I was there with you,
To make things right.
When you looked in my eyes,
And started to cry,
It did something to my heart,

And I thought it was time,
To ask you a question,
About you and me.
Maybe there's more than friends here,
Could there be a you and me.
Through all the things we've been through,
Supporting each other every day,
I want to tell you deep down,
But it scares me, what you might say.
I'm in love with you,
But it's hard to tell you so,
Because I don't know if it will ruin us.
As friends or lovers, what's better, I don't know.

I WISH I COULD CREATE ANOTHER YOU

As I walked through the rain today,
All I could think about was you.
The way we use to walk together,
The love we had was so true.
We raised our children and loved it all,
We both knew that we wouldn't fall.
Why did he ever call?
Now I don't have you at all.
Now I walk in the rain wondering what to do,
It hurts me every day,
Knowing that he is with you.
I don't have the kids,
And honey I'm blue,
I'm sitting here wondering,
I wish I could create another you.
Because I know if I had another you,
My life would be full again,
And the kids and I,
Would be your friend,
Instead of him.

BREATHLESS BEAUTY

It was like the sweet smell of orange blossoms,
And a soft summer breeze,
And floating through the meadow,
I was in heaven, it seemed to me.
There's no flower on earth,
With colors so bright and true,
That could match the beauty,
That I saw, when I saw you.
Your smile melted my heart,
Your warmth took my breath away,
Your voice like a choir of angels,
You left me breathless, with nothing to say.
After seeing you in your beauty,
Walking away was really hard,
And when I left you,
I left something with you, my heart.

A WONDERFUL CREATION

Like the morning dawn,
And the glistening dew,
The calm of the sea,
And the sky so blue.
The fall does come,
And so does the spring,
The beauty God made,
Are definite things.
The joy of the world,
The glorious sensation,
But I'll have to admit,
You are one of Gods better creations.

CHAPTER FIVE

These are some fun poems,
I told christopher, this is how
country and western songs are made.

TIME TO QUIT SINGING THE BLUES

I wish that I could quit singing the blues,
A country song or even rock, would stop me thinking of you.
You ruined my life and made me weak, you know,
I'd be better off girl, writing your name in the snow.
Cause that's how you treated me, like no one would see,
And then you walked out the door, you blamed everything on me.
You took my money, and took my friends,
Took my life, I know this won't end.
And everyone wonders, I wish I could quit sing the blues,
And I wish I could quit singing the blues.
A country song or even rock, would stop me thinking of you.
I did what I could, and thought I was right,
And I know you're in someones arms tonight.
I wish I could quit singing the blues.

WALK AWAY BLUES

I woke up this morning, and it was raining outside,
I reached looking for you, and you weren't by my side.
So I got up to make my coffee, and you took that too.
First you take my coffee, and now you make me blue.
That's why I woke up this morning, with the walk away blues.
I don't care what happens because it just don't include you.
You were my life, you were my song,
Why am I always so wrong?
I guess that's why I have these walk away blues.
I went to walk the dog, and found that blue was gone,
He had lots of food and water there, now what have I done?
I'm tired of being a slave, and I'm actually tired of you.
I'm so confused, I don't know what to do.
That's why I woke up this morning, with these walk away blues.
That's why I have these walk away blues.
I don't care what happens, because it just don't include you.
You were my life, and you were my song, why am I always wrong?
I guess that's why I have, these walk away blues.

WHY SHOULD YOU BE BLUE

Why should you be blue girl, you're the one that left me?
I've done everything I can for you, or did you ever see?
I would get home after work, and find that you weren't here,
Where could you be babe, hoping it's not my worst fear.
That you might just be, with someone new.
Now you're happy with him girl, so why should you be blue?
I'm the one who sits here, not knowing what to do,
While you're the one out partying it up, you two.
You have a good time, while I stay here singing the blues.
I'm the one hurting, why should you be blue?
Maybe he isn't the one, that really stole your heart,
Maybe in that heart of yours, you found we should not have part.
But now you've made your bed girl, and don't know what to do,

You hurt me bad, what should I do?
Why should you be blue?
You're the one that left me alone, and honey, I was true.
I'm the one that's hurting, why should you be blue?
Yes I'm the one that's hurting, why should you be blue?

GOT THE BLUES

Honey I've been sitting here, wondering why I got the blues,
Everything that I think about, has only to do with you.
You've been walking around, talking through the town,
About everything that we do.
Wonder what you're trying to say girl,
To make everyone think it's true.
I wonder if they know girl,
It only has to do with you.
You came into my heart,
And I saw life again,
It started like balls of fire,
And that's how fast it end.
Now, I seen you last night,
Talking to my friends,
You wouldn't even come over to me,
And I wondered if it would ever end.
How come you don't see me babe?
How come you really can't tell?
That I love you so much,
But you're really putting me through hell.
And now everybody wonders,
Why I sing the blues,
I wonder if they really know girl,
I t only has to do with you.
You came into my heart,
And I saw life again,
It started like balls of fire,
And that's how fast it end.

BLUE SKIES AND RAINY DAYS

I looked out the window today,
And saw blue skies looking back at me,
I didn't really know what I saw,
But it was nice to see.
Small clouds so white, and the sky being so blue,
Then it got dark, and it made me think of you.
Blue skies, rainy days, why did I ever think of you?
I went to the local market,
And bought a six pack to go,
I had the super bowl on tv,
And it was quite a show.
My team was winning,
And I was having a lot of fun,
I took a drink of beer, and it was flat.
It started raining, and I'm tired of that,
I can't even get rid of your cat,
Blue skies, rainy days,
Why did I ever think of you?

THOSE GETTING OVER YOU BLUES

Working so hard,
To go to work every day,
Trying to make a living,
And then I got fired today.
So I go to the local bar,
Where I know I have a lot of friends,
We party, we laugh,
We stay up till the night ends.
We talk real tough, we laugh real hard,
We even get in a fight or two,

But when I have an extra moment,
I always think of you,
You were so sweet,
And made my life,
And all night long,
I wish I was with you tonight.
So every night, and all day,
I always think about you,
And then I realize,
I have those getting over you blues.
You were the sweetest thing,
And I was so in love with you,
Then you left me alone babe,
And found somebody new.
I always treated you right,
And I will always love you,
So now I sit here at home girl,
Cause I got those getting over you blues.
Yeah, I got those getting over you blues again,
I wonder about you all the time,
And I wonder who's your new friend?
I don't even have a life,
And girl it ain't right,
That's why I always have those, getting over you blues.

BLUE CAUSE YOU MADE ME THAT WAY

I remember when I was so young, how it use to be,
I had all my friends over, they would never leave.
We had a lot of fun then, at least we thought so,
We planned on the next time, cause they knew they had to go.
And I'm blue, blue, blue, cause you made me that way,
I use to try to get rid of my friends, now I can't make them stay.
Can't even go down to the bar, and enjoy a drink or two,
Now I'm blue, blue, blue, and it's all because of you.
When I met you babe, you were the greatest thing,
The next thing I know girl, I need to buy you a ring,

We were doing so good, until I saw you with other guys,
Then it got pretty nasty, between you and I.
And I'm blue, blue, blue, because you made me that way,
I use to try to get rid of my friends, now I can't make them stay.
Can't even go down to the local bar, and have a drink or two,
Now I'm blue, blue, blue, and it's all because of you.
Now that you're with my friends, instead of me,
I don't even think about them, and how it use to be.
I'll just stay at home alone, and pass another day,
And I've really got the blues babe, cause you made me that way.
And I'm blue, blue, blue, because you made me that way,
I use to try to get rid of my friends, now I can't make them stay,
Can't even go down to the bar, and have a drink or two,
Now I'm blue, blue, blue, babe, and it's all because of you.

THOSE NOT WORKING BLUES

You know it's kinda nice,
Not having to work right now,
I don't have to break my back,
And putting up with things I don't allow.
I don't have to listen to the boss,
Try to tell me what to do.
I can stay here all day long babe,
Now it's just me and you.
You always told me hon,
That you wish I was home,
Now we have all this time girl,
For just you and me alone.
What do you mean, you have to go?
You have an appointment to keep?
I thought it would be romantic,
With just you and me.
Ok, it's fine, I'll see you later,
Who is that, that just drove up?
That's a fine-looking car,
I'll help you get your stuff.
I know you'll do fine dear,
At that meeting you're going to,
I' ll clean the house, and mow the lawn,
And honey, I'll be waiting for you.

I DON'T EVER GET PAID ON TIME

How come the company, can't pay me on time?
I work all week, and I know those hours are mine.
I get up at three, and I work till nine.
I tell my wife I'm working, she thinks I'm lying,
How come I can't ever get paid on time?
My rent is overdue, and they charge me for being late,
They put a lock on my door and say, we need to be paid.

You have to leave, you can't stay here no more,
I get home late from work, my wife's locked me out of the door.
How come I never get paid on time?
I know I'm doing good here, and you say I'm doing fine,
Everything you put me through here,
I think I ought to get paid on time.
I can't even look for another job,
Cause I don't have the gas, or the time.
I think I should be paid here,
And man it should be on time.
How come I can't even get paid on time?
I work all week and do a good job,
And I know those hours are mine,
I get up real early, and work real late,
If I was the boss, I wouldn't hesitate,
To make sure my boys, got paid on time.
It ain't right, and now I'm gonna fight,
To make sure I get paid on time.
Most guys I know, get paid weed to week,
I don't see them diving in dumpsters,
Looking for something to eat.
The kids all yell, and the fault is mine,
Because I'm the only one here,
That doesn't get paid on time.

IT'S NOT YOUR LIFE

This is not your life,
Why do you live it for me?
It's not your life,
When will you ever see?
I can do this on my own,
I can make it I know,
So stay out of my life
And leave me alone.
If you just believed in me,
And all the things I did,

Try helping me out here,
Instead of treating me like a kid.
Try to help me,
Instead of always putting me down,
Have a little faith in me,
And be positive, when you're around.
I can do this on my own,
And I can make it I know,
And I could do better,
If a little compassion, you show.
It's not your life,
Please leave me alone.

LANDSCAPE KING

As I drive in my truck, down street after street,
With mower in back, I know this job's right for me.
There are so many people, that need me out there,
To take care of their yards, cause they know I care.
Even their pets, like it when I show up,
Cause I give them water, when they don't have enough.
The neighbor next door, or the person across the street,
Wonder how come the yards I do, never has weeds.
The plants and lawn, are always green.
They think to themselves, maybe he'll work for me,
To make my yard look, as good as theirs,
And how much it cost, I really don't care.
Oh what a feeling to get my mower on the grass,
And then taking out my weed eater, and filling it with gas.
Trimming the hedges, and taking care of the plants,
Protecting the foliage, from snails and ants.
Making your yard look like a dream come true,
That's my business, and I'm here to satisfy you.
Yes, doing your yard, that's my thing,
And that's why they call me, The Landscape King.

CHAPTER SIX

TO MY SON CHRISTOPHER

I want to dedicate this book to my son Christopher, who joined the Lord July 4, of 1996. He had cancer at the age of 9, and was a fighter for 4 years. He made everyone smile, and always kept us on our toes. He loved music and going out for pizza. He also loved the Lord and proclaimed Him until his death in 1996. He was a strong boy and always knew what was going on. And he has been the inspiration for this book. He loved listening to my music and loved all the different types of poems I wrote, whether Christian, love, or just fun poems or songs. He was a big inspiration for my new Christian CD, (Kirk In Spirit), which is now available. A young boy who didn't really have a chance in life, but he enjoyed it to the fullest. That's why this book is about him, he was there and helped me with all that was written in it, because he just plain enjoyed life, and he helped us to do the same.

I have some poems that are about Christopher in Chapter 3. And these next three writings are what his mom and his two sisters wrote after Christopher joined the Lord.

We all love and miss you Christopher, you were and still are a great inspiration to all the people that your heart touched, which was many people.

We will meet you in heaven.

In memory of Christopher Alan Melton, Philipsen

Nov. 26, 1982- July 4, 1996

THIS IS WHAT CHRISTOPHER'S MOM VICKIE WROTE AFTER HIS PASSING

He was so young God,
so young and strong, and filled with promise.
So vital, so radiant, giving so much joy wherever he went.
He was so brilliant, on this one boy You lavished so many
talents that could have enriched your world. He had already
received so many honors, and there were so many honors to come.
Why then? In our agony we ask, why him? Why not someone less
gifted? Someone less good, some hop-headed rioter, thief, brute, hood?
Yet we know even as we demand what seems to us a rational answer,
that we are only intensifying our grief. Plunging deeper in the blind and
witless place where all hope is gone.
You will always be in our hearts, we love you Christopher.

THIS IS WHAT CHRISTOPHER'S SISTER KATI, WROTE AFTER HIS PASSING

Oh Christopher Alan
It was about wintertime, when the rain was pounding,
That Christopher Alan was diagnosed with luekemia,
Cancer an experience that had hearts crashing.
He was sent down through the town to every doctor,
To see if he would progress from day to day.
Oh live if you may, Oh Christopher Alan.
Slowly, slowly, his body gave, weaker and weaker, he became.
His family searched for hope, not knowing how to cope.
Oh sick, he is very, very sick, poor Christopher Alan,
Oh the better death may be for you, but my hearts blood is spilling.
Oh don't you remember brother, when you were a normal boy?
Playing happily on the merry-go-round?
But now you're dangerously sick, Oh Christopher Alan.
His face turned a yellow, and death was his dealing,
May everyone remember him for, Oh Christopher Alan will soon have a calling.

Slowly, slowly, the Lord raised him up, piece by piece he left.
His family cried and screamed, but still supported him in near time of death.
It had not been days, but years, until the Lord took him, and he was gone.
The call for this young child had increased,
The family's pain as they mourned for Christopher Alan.
Oh mother, Oh father, he is gone, and his body is lifeless,
His soul is in my heart, my brother died today,
But I'll live life for him everyday, Oh Christopher Alan.

I love and miss you Christopher
Love Kati

THIS IS WHAT CHRISTOPHER'S SISTER DAWN WROTE AFTER HIS PASSING

To My Brother Christopher

I was young then and didn't fully understand, but now I'm grown and realize you got dealt an unfair hand. The fight for your life started the day you were born, you were so tiny, yet so strong, and you pulled through. Everything wasokay until you were nine. They diagnosed you with brain tumors and eventually cancer. Your fight to live was and still is what inspired me today. It kills me inside to think back now as an adult and fully realize what you had to endure. All the medicines chemo, shots, and pain, as your everyday life you were and still are amazing to me. Always loved life, always so happy, and always thinking of others, touching the hearts of many even when your life was a constant battle, you are amazing. At times I was selfish and didn't say the things I wish so bad I could say today. I always looked up to you, you were my big brother, our protector. You fought for life, for mom, dad, Kati, and me, and we fought for you. But after four years of fighting, your poor mind, body, and soul, couldn't fight anymore. It was a very sad, sad, 4th of July in 1996. Under all my sadness I was so happy for you. It was your Independence Day from all the torture and pain. I love and miss you so much and wish everyday things could have been different for you, but I am so happy you are in a better place free from any pain. And I know you are shining down on us protecting *us everyday. I can't wait for the day I get to see you again, until then, you will always and forever be in my heart, I love you so much.*

Always and Forever,
You sister, Dawn

ABOUT THE AUTHOR

I was born and raised in Southern California. I have two brothers and two sisters. We had a quite unique life, because most of it involved music. My grandmother played piano for the first silent movies, and she also played guitar, fiddle, and other instruments. My uncle was considered one of the best drummers around, and even recorded some of those old 45 records, or was it 78? Some of my other uncles also recorded songs. Our family was close and we both loved, and respected each other. My mom was the hub of it all, and she was and always will be my inspiration in life. It was a very close and happy life we lived. Until in 1964 we found out that my mom had cancer. She never showed us kids that she was hurting or having a bad day or anything, as a matter of fact, I don't even remember my mom and dad ever even argue. Then while I was in the Navy, at 19 years old, I was called home because my mom wasn't doing well. It ended up that she passed away to the Lord in 1969 at 39 years old. My mom and dad had been married for 25 years, and all of us kids knew nothing else than love from them both.

So we kept going and we still kept playing and singing music. It has been very hard for all of us, but we knew she was with the Lord, and wasn't in pain anymore. In my first marriage I was blessed with three wonderful children. My second marriage I was also blessed with three wonderful children. I worked as a foreman or a superintendent most of the years as a rebar Ironworker. But things took a turnabout in 1992 when my son from my second marriage, Christopher, was having pains in his stomach. I took him to the doctor and later that day they called me and wanted us to come in right away. We did and that's when they told me they want to do further testing because of his blood cell count. They retested and the results came back positive for ALL-Leukemia, and he also had brain tumors, and my heart just melted in my chest. Christopher at that time was 9 years old.

They put him on a regiment of medications, and appointments. This all became a lot of stress for me, him, his mom, and his two sisters. The doctors told me that if he can make it four years in remission, that he would be out of the woods. So for four years we were doing the Chemo and doctor's appointments, I can't remember how many, plus all the radiation for his brain tumors. Finally, four years came and the doctor told us that he was out of the woods, you could imagine the relief and joy we all had. Later on, that day they called me and said that we need to talk, and I should come in right away, and bring Christopher. They told me that Christopher had a relapse, and there is nothing they can do. Within two months Christopher passed away to be with the Lord, he was thirteen years young. That is what has inspired me to write the poems I did about him, and there are more but it is just too hard to re-live all of the feelings and thoughts.

After that it was the hardest time, I ever have had in my whole life. The only thing that kept me sane and not being very hateful, was the fact of knowing that Christopher was with the Lord, He had His reasons, and I was humble enough to accept that. And it has made me a lot stronger in the Lord.

I just remember the times that we had with Christopher and how strong and brave he was through all of this. He loved being around all the music, the pizza, and all the things that we all did together.

Within that year my youngest daughter, at 9 years old started losing her hair, she had beautiful long, curly, blonde hair. And then she was diagnosed with Alopecia Universalis, and ended up losing all of her hair, everywhere. She was teased and had a horrible time in school. I finally took her out of public school, and she ended up finishing her schooling at a private school.

Now everyone is getting their own lives together, they all have good jobs and their own families.

I was injured on the job in 1992, when I was hit in the head by a 500-pound commercial freezer door that fell, no fault of my own. So needless to say, I became disabled and can't work. It took a long time for me to get use to not being able to do much, but after a few years I adjusted, which brings me to what I'm doing now. No, my life hasn't been all bad, actually I am very happy with my total life.

Through all the things I've been through, I've learned a lot (of course I hear age does the same thing), but it has lead me to this book, and my new CD Kirk In Spirit that has just been released. And I have my own company as a new record label called Blu Streets Records. And a really good relationship with Jesus Christ, which is my everything now.

Plus, I wouldn't change things, you know the saying, I could have missed the pain, but I would have missed the dance.

So that is why I decided to use the things that the Lord has gifted me with and publish this book, and complete my new Christian CD.

And I decided to dedicate this book to Christopher, and we will be caught up with him, as we are lifted up to meet the Lord, Amen.

Christopher Alan Melton, Philipsen
Nov. 26, 1982 – July 4th 1996

These are the links to my new Christian Praise CD

Kirk In Spirit
http://www.blustreetsrecords.com
http://www.kirkphilipsen.com
http://www.cdbaby,com/cd/kirkphilipsen6

Kirk's Poetry

Thank You for your patronage

www.ingramcontent.com/pod-product-compliance
Lightning Source LLC
Chambersburg PA
CBHW051246120626
46547CB00014B/1817